A BRIEF READER ON THE VIRTUES OF THE HUMAN HEART

JOSEF PIEPER

A BRIEF READER
ON THE VIRTUES OF
THE HUMAN HEART

Translated by
Paul C. Duggan

IGNATIUS PRESS   SAN FRANCISCO

Originally published in German as
Kleines Lesebuch
von den Tugenden des menschlichen Herzens
© 1988 Schwabenverlag AG
Ostfildern bei Stuttgart

Cover design by Roxanne Mei Lum
Cover border by Pamela Kennedy
Calligraphy by Victoria Hoke Lane

With ecclesiastical approval
© 1991 Ignatius Press, San Francisco
All rights reserved
ISBN 978-0-89870-303-0
Library of Congress Catalogue number 90–81767
Printed in the United States of America

A RETROSPECTIVE PREFACE

In Reinhold Schneider's elegiac autobiography (*Verhüllter Tag* [The veiled day]) there is a chapter with the heading "Colmar". It begins with his complaint that as a writer he no longer had "any legal prospects" in Germany. The publishing house Insel-Verlag had just informed him that then in 1941 only "books necessary and important for the war effort" were permitted. As it turned out, an unexpected new opportunity emerged in the Alsatia-Verlag in Colmar. Inevitably he came to speak with the director of that publishing house, "a man laden with troubles". "Just as the accent on his name, Rosse or Rossé, shifted back and forth, so did his political situation shift. . . . Joseph Rossé could be a hero tomorrow and a traitor again the day after tomorrow." There then follows a brief account of the three-time incarceration of this man. The first one, even before the war, overtook him as a provocatively resolute Alsatian. From his second imprisonment, imposed upon him for the same reasons as the first while war broke out, he was liberated by German troops. Finally, he was sentenced as a *collaborateur* to fifteen years' hard labor in a penitentiary in the Pyrenees; he did not survive that confinement.

Reinhold Schneider, his author, who in the meantime became his friend, says that "amid bitter suffering and anxiety, but consoled by God, he died as one of the elect".

It so happened that this man, Joseph Rossé, about whose fate I first learned something during the fifties from Reinhold Schneider's book, was the director of the same publishing house for which I became an author at the same time in 1941; this occurred through the almost chance mediation of a friend, without my being at all aware of the connections.

For myself as well, at that time there was no more opportunity for my activity as a writer. In the index of my works that was published in 1974, for the time between 1940 and 1948 only two books are listed, and both of them were brought into print by that same publisher in Colmar. To be sure, only one of them was "published", namely, this newly issued *Brief Reader* from 1941. The other book, *Wahrheit der Dinge,*[1] was indeed printed, in an edition of ten thousand copies. Not one of them, however, appeared in public light, since the entire lot burned up amid the storms of war that advanced on Colmar in 1944. This mis-

---

[1] *The Truth of All Things* in *Living the Truth* (San Francisco: Ignatius Press, 1989).

fortune proved later to harbor an unexpected stroke of luck: in 1945, as I returned from confinement as a prisoner of war, I thereby had available an "as yet unpublished" *Habilitationsschrift* (post-doctoral thesis) to submit to the University of Münster. However, that is a new and different story about which no more will be said here.

Nevertheless, it is to be remarked that here in Germany at that time one hardly knew anything about the factual conditions and still less about the unusually dramatic and plainly tragic circumstances under which the operations of the Alsatia-Verlag were conducted. On the contrary, it was said that the National Socialist regime favored the German-Alsatian publisher with these exceptional—and, for us, surprising—allocations of paper out of purely political calculation. In reality, things were very different. Indeed, the director of the firm was awarded some party honors that to him were most undesirable. The paper allocations, however, were the work of an influential friend in Berlin, who, despite the category of "strictly illegal", did the right thing with the utmost daring. And in the Colmar publishing house one carried on in constant expectation of a shutdown by the Nazi regime, particularly because of the persistently exclusive production of plainly Christian religious literature. There is still a third

coworker to be mentioned, one who labored in secret in the "Church war aid": he saw to it that all these "undesirable" writings, as had been already done earlier with the brief edition of the "Christian Primer", were provided with the official stamp of the "responsible" political offices and placed on the list of officially permitted literature for mass distribution on the front lines.

It is, then, the purpose of this retrospective to place a modest monument to this concealed and unselfish yet, to put it mildly, still unthanked deed.

J. P.

Virtue is the utmost of what a man can be; it is the realization of the human capacity for being.

The primal will for the good lives from the ongoing momentum of the original leap by which man, in answer to the creative call of God, crossed over the chasm that divides nothingness from existence. This is the momentum with which the possible rushes forth into the radiant early morning of its first realization: the flow of a stream that has its source in the bright darkness of the natural and, ever nourished by its origin, attains the brink of the realm of freedom under the judgment of the primal conscience.

The luminous domain of free human action, governed by knowledge, is ringed on all sides by the darkness, the darkness of the natural in us and the deeper impenetrable darkness of the immediately divine rule of our desire and action. Yet both areas are dark only to us. In reality, they are irradiated by the unending brightness of divine knowledge and foresight. Concerning this brightness, Sacred Scripture says that its "light" is "inaccessible" (1 Tim 6:16); according to Aristotle, our understanding relates to it "as the eyes of nocturnal birds to the light of day".

The strain of self-mastery, which for us country-men of Kant is inseparable from any concept of upbringing and moderation and is generally tied to and fused with the concept of virtue, is an accompanying phenomenon only of less perfect and beginner stages, whereas authentic, perfected virtue, by dint of the very definition of the concept, bears the happily radiant seal of spontaneity, of freedom from constraint and of self-evident inclination.

Thomas Aquinas, the great teacher of Western Christianity, endeavored to express the Christian image of man in seven theses, which can be summarized in the following manner:

First: the Christian is one who, in *faith*, becomes aware of the reality of the triune God. Second: the Christian strives, in *hope*, for the total fulfillment of his being in eternal life. Third: the Christian directs himself, in the divine virtue of *love*, to an affirmation of God and neighbor that surpasses the power of any natural love. Fourth: the Christian is *prudent*; namely, he does not allow his view on reality to be controlled by the Yes or No of his will, but rather he makes this Yes or No of the will dependent upon the truth of real things. Fifth: the Christian is *just*; that is, he is able to live "with the other" in truth; he sees himself as a member

among members of the Church, of the people, and of any community. Sixth: the Christian is *brave*, that is, he is prepared to suffer injury and, if need be, death for the truth and for the realization of justice. Seventh: the Christian is *temperate*; namely, he does not permit his desire to possess and his desire for pleasure to become destructive and inimical to his being.

All duty is based upon being. Reality is the basis of ethics. Goodness is the standard of reality. Whoever wants to know and do the good must direct his gaze toward the objective world of being, not toward his own "sentiment" or toward arbitrarily established "ideals" and "models". He must look away from his own deed and look upon reality.

The "soundness" of justice, of fortitude, of temperance, of fear of the Lord and of virtue in general lies in the fact that they are appropriate to objective reality, both natural and supernatural. Conformity to reality is the principle of both soundness and goodness.

The precedence of prudence indicates that the realization of goodness presumes knowledge of reality.

Whatever is good is ascertained by prudence; in turn, whatever is prudent is established by the "thing itself". Reality, grasped in knowledge, is not only the first given from which the freely desiring outreach of man into the world takes its beginning: at the same time it is also the last point of appeal for the retrospective justification of this outreach inside a person.

To the mind of contemporary man, the concept of goodness is excluded rather than included in the concept of prudence. For him there is no good deed that cannot be imprudent or evil deed that cannot be prudent: rather often he will judge lying and cowardice to be prudent but truthfulness and brave self-denial just as often to be imprudent. In contrast, the classical and Christian doctrine of living states that man is prudent and good only together; prudence belongs to the definition of the good. There is no justice or fortitude that can contradict the virtue of prudence; anyone who is unjust is also imprudent through and through. *Omnis virtus moralis debet esse prudens*: all virtue is necessarily prudent.

Only someone who is silent is listening. And only the invisible is transparent. To be sure, a deeper

silence than mere abstention from speech and utterance is required. There is also interior speech which must also become mute, so things might find their proper utterance.

Thus, one who is truly listening is not "deadening" himself into an unnatural and unintellectual dumbness. His silence is also by no means an empty and dead soundlessness. In this silence there is not only listening but also answering. What the true listener forbids himself is simply this: neither to obscure the radiance of his own eye that gazes on the sun nor to allow the soul's ability to answer (wherein lies its closest cor-"respondence" to the Source of Being) to lapse into words.

Thus, the world reveals itself to the silent listener and only to him; the more silently he listens, the more purely is he able to perceive reality.

Since reason is nothing else than the power to understand reality, then all reasonable, sensible, sound, clear, and heart-stirring talk stems from listening silence. Thus all discourse requires a foundation in the motherly depth of silence. Otherwise speech is sourceless: it turns into chatter, noise, and deception.

We lose our speech not only when we are forced down below the threshold of our being but also when we are raised up above our capacities.

The core of human existence, the cultivated field of word and speech, thus borders on the right and on the left with wordlessness: with the muteness of the infant and the muteness of the mystic. Talk, however, sets its roots downward into the nourishing soil of silence.

A particular form of nonsilence has always been regarded as a kin of despair: talkativeness, babble, the unquenchable frenzy of idle talk. When, however, talk of this kind, which one encounters truly everywhere in the workplace and the marketplace as a constant temptation, when such deafening talk, literally bent upon thwarting listening, appears to be connected with hopelessness—it is to be asked, then, should there not be in silence, in listening silence, necessarily a drop of hope? Who indeed could be attentive in silence to the discourse of things unless he expected something from perceiving the truth? And in a newly established discipline of silence, would there not lie the chance not only of overcoming the sterility of everyday talk but also its kin, hopelessness—even if perhaps at first only insofar as we acknowledged the true face of this kinship? I realize that other faculties, applied to human purposes, come into play here; perhaps the circle has to be broken at some other point. Nonetheless, one may ask whether

the "quick strict resolution" to keep silence could at the same time be a kind of exercise in hope?

Wherever the arts live from the festive contemplation of the world and its foundations, something like a liberation is achieved, a setting forth under the open sky—both for the creative artist himself as well as for the simplest onlooker. A man needs this liberation, this presentiment of the final and utmost stillness, almost more than he needs bread, which is indispensable and yet insufficient.

Prudence, as the formal basis and "birth mother" of all human virtue, is the cautious and decisive faculty of our spirit for shaping things, which transforms the knowledge of reality into the accomplishment of the good. It encompasses the humility of silent, i.e., unbiased, understanding, memory's faithfulness to being, the art of letting things speak for themselves, the alert composure before the unexpected. Prudence means the hesitant seriousness and, so to speak, the filter of reflection and yet also the daring courage for definitive resolution. It means cleanness, uprightness, openness, and impartiality of the being, elevated above all difficulties and expediencies of the merely "tactical".

Prudence, as Paul Claudel says, is the "knowing bow" of our being, as it must be steered through a multiplicity of limitations into perfection.

In the virtue of prudence the ring of active life is closed and rounded to its genuine fulfillment: out of the experience of reality the person works toward reality, thus realizing himself in decision and action. This condition manifests its depth in the singular utterance of Thomas Aquinas: in prudence, the dominant virtue of the conduct of our lives, the happiness of active life is resolved.

Prudence its that lamp of moral existence of which it is said in one of the wisest books of the East that it is denied to anyone who "regards himself". There is a dark resolution and a bright resolution: prudence is the brightness of the resolution of the one who has decided "to live by the truth" (Jn 3:21).

The finite spirit is not so deeply understandable to itself or powerful over itself that it can follow only its own light in all things. Nor is it sovereign over objective realities, unlike a field commander with a comprehensive view; rather, it is urged and compelled by its nature to learn the truth about objective realities. However, the path that this urging, separate from any self-determination, follows is illumined by that dim light that completely

envelops and surrounds the clear vessel of our self-governing freedom.

Nonetheless, it remains true for this sphere of free action that man's good lies in being in accordance with reason.

The man who does good follows the lines of an architectural plan that has not been devised by himself or even totally understood by himself in all its components. This plan is revealed to him moment by moment only through a narrow cleft and a tiny gap; in his transient condition, he never perceives the specific plan for himself in its global and definitive form. Concerning conscience, which to an extent is prudence itself, Paul Claudel says that it is the "forbearing lamp that characterizes for us not the future but the immediate".

Man's moral deeds are not more or less identifiable handholds as he scales the heights of technical accomplishment but rather are steps in his self-realization. The human self, which grows toward its fulfillment by performing the good, is a "work" that surpasses from the very beginning all human plans and designs. The becoming of the moral person occurs in the individual's appropriate response to reality, which we have not made and whose essence is the shifting forms of becom-

ing and perishing but not permanent being (only God is He Who Is).

To know the final goals of one's own life is not and cannot be the fruit of a knowledge to be sought and completed still in this "lifetime". The goals are declared. No one is unaware that one must love and do the good; everyone knows — explicitly or not — that the distinctive good of man is "to be in accordance with reason", that is, to be in accordance with one's own reality and with reality that one has helped to shape; and there is no one to whom it must still be said that one must be just and courageous and temperate; for all this, no "reflection" is needed.

Moral virtue, insofar as it is the basic attitude of voluntary affirmation of the good, is the foundation and precondition of prudence. Yet prudence is the prerequisite for the appropriate realization and effect of this basic attitude here and now. One can be prudent only if one loves and wills the good through and through; indeed, only one who is first prudent can do good. Since, however, the love for good grows over and over through doing, the foundations of prudence are the more deepened and strengthened the more that it is fruitful.

There is an amazing and scarcely fathomable depth in this sentence of Thomas Aquinas: false prudence and excessive cleverness are derived from and essentially tied to covetousness.

This statement puts the virtue of prudence itself and the basic human attitude operative in it into a sharp new light; it includes the fact that prudence is opposed to covetousness in a most particular way. With one stroke a nexus among several strands of thought is suddenly exposed, thoughts that previously did not seem to be connected.

Moreover the German language, with a memory that is no longer distinct, seems to be aware of that secret tie between covetousness and false prudence, a fact that by itself is just as surprising. In Low German the one and the same word *wies* stands for both the prudent as well as the covetous; and the Middle High German word *karg* (*karc*), meaning the clever cunning of selfishness, is considered as falling well within prudence's range of meaning and its "verbal field".

"Covetousness" here means more than the disordered love for money and property. Covetousness is to be understood here as the immoderate striving after all "possessions", through which the person thinks he can assure his own greatness and

worth. Covetousness thus signifies the anxious se-
nility of a frantic self-preservation bent on only its
own assurance and security. Is further explanation
needed on how greatly all this is contrary to the innermost direction of prudence; how impossible it
is for one to have that silence that knows and recognizes the truth of objective realities; and how
impossible it is to have any conformity to reality
in knowing and deciding, without the youthfulness of a courageously trusting and, as it were,
prodigal renunciation of the conditions of anxious
self-preservation and of all selfish "interest" in
mere self-confirmation; how simply impossible,
then, is the virtue of prudence without the constant readiness for disregarding oneself and without the detachment and tranquility of authentic
humility and objectivity?

Even the highest supernatural prudence can have
no other meaning than this: to allow the more
deeply experienced truth of the reality of God and
of the world to become the measure and standard
for one's own desire and action. Indeed, never can
there be a norm for man other than Being itself as
well as Truth, whereby Being is revealed; and
there can be no higher norm for man than simply
God, who simply is, along with his truth.

Moreover, concerning the person who "does the truth", it is said in Sacred Scripture that he "comes to the light".

The basic attitude of conformity to being, of impartiality, and of objectivity, which is expressed in the classical teaching on prudence, was summarized in the Middle Ages in the marvelously simple sentence, "A man is wise when all things taste to him as they really are." There is a practical lesson from modern psychology, or rather modern "psychotherapy", that in my opinion can scarcely be taken seriously enough: namely, that a person, to whom things do not taste as they really are but who tastes only himself in all things because he has regard only for himself—that such a person not only has lost any real potentiality for justice (and for any moral virtue at all) but also has lost his psychological health—indeed, that a whole category of psychological illnesses is based substantially upon this selfish "subjectivity".

The prerequisite for justice is truth. Whoever rejects the truth, whether natural or supernatural, is at that point truly "evil" and unrepentant.

It happens that precisely the highest of man's natural abilities, namely, the cardinal virtue of pru-

dence, with a view to the supernatural new life's order of being within grace, conceals within itself the most dangerous possibilities of conflict and estrangement. Here the more universal law applies, in virtue of which the highest natural powers, not just the lowest, are capable of the most negative opposition to the divine. Yet of course the contrary is also true: the greatest and most fruitful effects occur precisely and only when the utmost and the supreme power of man's nature willingly submits and weds itself to the transforming core power of the new life. Only when the person's natural power, liberated from all fear of restriction, comes before the face of the Other, will his own depth of being be totally visible.

That one man gives to another what belongs to the other is the basis of all just order in the world. In contrast, all injustice means that what belongs to someone is either withheld or taken from him, not indeed by misfortune, bad harvest, fire or earthquake but by man.

Since the beloved is not properly "somebody else", justice does not formally exist between lovers. To be just means to acknowledge someone in case one cannot love him. Justice says that there is the other who is not like me but who nevertheless

is entitled to what is his. The just person is therefore just in that he confirms the other in his other-
ness and assists him toward that which belongs to
him.

That the fundamental act of commutative justice
is called "restitution" implies that it is not possible
to achieve a definitive ideal condition among men.
Rather, it means that the temporary, the non-
definitive and provisional, the repeated mere "im-
provement" in all historical action belongs to the
foundations of man and his world; thus the claim
to erect an imperturbable permanent order in the
world must necessarily lead to something inhuman.

The holder of governmental power can in fact not
be compelled to fulfill his duty of justice—since by
nature he himself is the protector and the agent of
distributive justice: "The ruler has his position in
order to protect justice." But if the protector of
justice does indeed not protect it? Then, dread-
fully, injustice takes place! And no appeal to ab-
stract jurisdictions such as "the conscience of
humanity", "world public opinion", or "history"
can change anything about it. Anyone who thinks
through this structural plan of *iustitia distributiva*
from the foundation up has to perceive what gov-

ernmental rule really is, and that in the human world there is hardly any worse or more hopeless calamity than unjust governmental rule.

The just man, the more he realizes that he is the recipient of gifts and that he has an obligation to God and to man, will alone be ready to fulfill what he does not owe. He will decide to give something to the other that no one can force him to give.

It is good to be forewarned that the mightiest embodiment of evil in human history, the Antichrist, could indeed appear in the form of a great ascetic. In point of fact, this is the nearly universal lesson of Western historical thought. One who does not grasp the fact and the reason that the worst corruption of the natural man is injustice has to come to ruin through the experiences that call attention to themselves in such visions amid a disorder that can scarcely be overcome. Above all, he would be incapable of recognizing the historical prefigures of that final condition; while he is looking out for the powers of corruption in a mistaken direction, they establish their rule before his eyes.

Fortitude presumes vulnerability; without vulnerability there is no possibility of fortitude. An angel cannot be courageous because it is not vulnerable.

To be brave means to be ready to sustain a wound. Since he is substantially vulnerable, man can be courageous.

Every wound of the natural being tends toward death. Thus every brave deed draws sustenance from preparedness for death as from its deepest root, even though, when viewed from outside, it might appear far removed from any thought about death. A "fortitude" that does not extend to the depth of readiness to fall is rotten in its root and lacking in effective power.

Willingness to be wounded constitutes only the half, the part in the forefront of fortitude. The courageous person is not willing to sustain a wound for its own sake. Rather, through it he wants to protect or gain a deeper, more substantial freedom from harm.

To be brave is not the same as to have no fear. To be sure, fortitude excludes a certain kind of fearlessness, namely, when it is based on a mistaken appraisal and evaluation of reality. This sort of fearlessness either is blind and deaf toward actual danger or else stems from a reversal in love. For fear and love limit one another: one who does not love does not fear either, and one who loves falsely

also fears falsely. Anyone who has lost the will to live does not fear death. This dispirited indifference, however, is remote from authentic fortitude; it is a reversal of the natural order. Fortitude apprehends, acknowledges, and protects the natural order of things. The brave person is perceptive: he realizes that the wound he gets is an evil. He does not falsify reality or alter its value: it "tastes" to him as it really is. He does not love death, nor does he despise life.

That person is brave who does not allow himself to be brought by the fear of secondary and transient evils to the point of forsaking the final and authentic good things and thus of taking on himself the ultimate and unlimited horror. This fear of the definitive terror belongs, as the "negative" of love for God, to the plainly necessary foundation of fortitude (and of any virtue): "The man who fears the Lord will not be fainthearted" (Sir 34:14).

Fortitude presumes to a certain extent that a man is afraid of evil; its essence does not consist in knowing no fear but rather in not allowing himself to be compelled by fear into evil or to fail to accomplish the good. Anyone who ventures into some danger, even for the sake of the good, without realizing how dangerous it is, or out of an im-

pulsive optimism ("Nothing is going to happen to me"), or with a well-founded confidence in his own power and capacity for struggle does not yet have the virtue of fortitude. The possibility of being courageous in the true sense comes about only when all those apparent or genuine elements of security fail, that is, when the natural man fears for himself: indeed, not when he fears for himself out of baseless anxiety, but rather when, on the basis of clear perception of the true state of matters, he cannot do otherwise—as it were, with good reason—but fear for himself. Whoever in such a situation of unqualified seriousness, in the face of which any *miles gloriosus* (glorious soldier) falls mute and every heroic gesture becomes crippled, nonetheless advances toward the horror and does not allow himself to be prevented from doing the good, specifically for the sake of the good and thus finally for the sake of God, not out of ambition or out of fear of being taken for a coward: that person is truly courageous.

What is essential to the virtue of fortitude is not aggression or self-confidence or wrath but rather steadfastness and patience. This, however—and this point cannot be repeated too frequently—is not because patience and steadfastness are simply better and more perfect than aggressiveness and

self-confidence but rather because the real world is
so structured that it is in the most extreme emer-
gency, where the only resistance possible is steadfastness, that the final and most profound spiritual
strength of the person can become manifest.

Patience is not the indiscriminate acceptance of
any sort of evil: "It is not the one who does not flee
from evil who is patient but rather the one who
does not let himself thereby be drawn into disordered sadness." To be patient means not to allow
the serenity and discernment of one's soul to be
taken away. Patience, then, is not the tear-
streaked mirror of a "broken" life (as one might
almost think, to judge from what is frequently
shown and praised under this term) but rather is
the radiant essence of final freedom from harm.
Patience is, as Hildegard of Bingen states, "the pil-
lar that is weakened by nothing".

The virtue of fortitude protects a person from lov-
ing his life in such a way that he loses it.

The Christian prototype of the "heroic downfall"
is the testimony of blood, the martyr's death. It is
characterized by the fact that in it the greatest
readiness for suffering, which is able to forego
even the "heroic", is immediately bound with the

affirmation of the highest worth and of the highest reality. The same can be said concerning the foundation of Christian readiness for suffering, namely, concerning asceticism. And even the seemingly senseless downfall along with the seemingly senseless suffering contains for the Christian believer a mystery-filled opportunity for the affirmation of being in itself: namely, the opportunity of devotion to the community of the suffering Son of Man. Yet these are matters that one cannot discuss with a non-Christian, and it would be good to subject them again to some sort of "arcane discipline".

The virtue of fortitude has nothing to do with a purely vital, blind pluck (even though it greatly requires healthy vital organs, more so perhaps than any other virtue). The one who puts himself in harm's way uncritically and indiscriminately is not brave; this merely shows that he places more value uncritically and indiscriminately on all kinds of things than he does on his personal security, which he places at risk for these things. Not just any giving of oneself for anything amounts to the essence of fortitude but rather only a giving of oneself that corresponds to reason, namely, to the true essence and value of real things. True fortitude requires a correct appreciation of things, both

of those that one "risks" as well as those that one
hopes to protect or to gain through one's effort.
The Greek panegyric that Pericles included in the
elevated words of his speech for the fallen ex-
presses what is also Christian wisdom: "For this is
our manner: to take the greatest risks where we
have thought matters through most carefully.
Among others, however, only ignorance pro-
duces bravery, while reflection causes trembling."

Without a "just cause" there is no fortitude. The
decisive element is not the wound but the cause.
"A man does not expose his life to the danger of
death except in order to secure justice. Therefore
praise for bravery is contingent upon justice",
says Thomas Aquinas. And in his book *On Duties*,
Ambrose says, "Courage without justice is a lever
of evil."

For the moral virtue of fortitude, the old tenet of
classical Western rules for living holds true: every
virtue must always be tied with all others at their
core; thus there can be no bravery without truthfulness, without justice, or without discipline. It is
a bourgeois illusion to think that a person can be
just without ever being required to demonstrate
his courage as well. It is no less a distortion of
meaningful order to believe that one can be brave
even though he knowingly fights on the side of

injustice; the bravery of the criminal is a contradic-
tion in terms. Likewise, fortitude as a moral virtue
can have no bond with indiscipline; In *Parcival* it is
said, "Never have I heard that a man was praised
for undisciplined bravery."

Discipline is selfless self-preservation. Indiscipline
is self-destruction through selfish debasement of
powers intended for self-preservation.

It is an everyday but no less mysterious fact that
the interior order of a man is not—unlike glass, a
flower, or a beast—a merely given and obvious reality but rather that those same powers by which
human existence sustains itself could subvert that
interior order even to the point of the destruction
of the spiritual moral person. It is especially hard
to conceive that it is truly the innermost human
self that can bring itself to self-destruction in disorder. Man indeed is not a battlefield of conflicting
powers and drives that vanquish one another; further, it is only a picturesque and inexact manner of
speaking that sensuality "in us" defeats reason.
Rather, we ourselves alone are always the agents
of discipline and indiscipline, of self-preservation
and self-destruction. The interior order is either
protected or distorted always by the decisive cen-
ter of the entire and indivisible person: "The evil I
do not want is what I do" (Rom 7:19).

All discipline aims toward the person of the very one who carries it out. This direction is, of course, always in danger of losing its selflessness, of going astray into frenzied pomposity, and of drawing from ascetic "successes" the payoff of a firm self-admiration. Vanity, self-importance, impatient arrogance over the "deficient people"—these are the specific perils of the ascetic. In his "Shepherd's Rule", an inexhaustible treasury of wisdom for living, Gregory the Great expressed this clearly. Cheerfulness of the heart, moreover, is the seal of selflessness. By this seal one recognizes with certainty that hypocrisy and any frenzy of self-absorption are very remote. Cheerfulness of the heart is the unmistakable sign through which the inner authenticity of discipline as selfless self-preservation becomes manifest.

The customary notion of "moderation" dwells in fatal proximity to the fear of any exuberance. Everybody knows what the saying "everything with moderation" (which surely can have a lofty meaning) means in everyday speech, and that the phrase "prudent moderation" especially applies when the love of truth or some other noble virtue of the heart is ready and eager to dare the utmost.

Discipline, states Ernst Jünger in his noteworthy essay "Uber den Schmerz" (On pain), has no other meaning than this: to keep life in uninterrupted contact with pain and thus to remain prepared to be "put into service at any time for the purposes of a higher order". To be sure, Jünger's rigid masklike concept of "discipline" is thoroughly distinct from the Christian notion of discipline and moderation; Jünger could never ratify the opinion of Thomas Aquinas that "the goal and norm of discipline is bliss". Nevertheless it appears that when one regards the Christian concept of discipline from the perspective of the fact of pain, behind its foreground of gladness over creation there lies a harder countenance, shaped by the decision to relinquish creation for the sake of its Creator—although even this harder countenance shines with an affirming cheerfulness that is infinitely superior to any naïve gladness over creation.

Temperance is not, in the strict and final sense, the "realization" of the good. Discipline and moderation and chastity are not in themselves the fulfillment of man. Temperance, insofar as it keeps the person himself in order by vigilance and restraint, provides for both the realization of one's own

good and the authentic progress of a man toward his goal, the unalterable requirement. Without it the stream of the innermost essential human will could overflow its banks, lose its direction, and never reach the sea of fulfillment. Yet temperance is not itself the stream. Still, it is the bank and rampart, and through its firmness the stream is endowed with an unhindered course, momentum, slope, and velocity.

The common Christian thinking, whenever there is a question of anger, seeks only to point out the unruly, the unspiritual, and the negative in anger. Still, just like "sensuality" and "desire", the power of becoming angry belongs to the basic powers of man. In this power of becoming angry the energy of human nature speaks most clearly. This power is aimed at what is hard to achieve, at that which eludes easy grasp; it is always readily available where a *bonum arduum*, a difficult good, waits to be won.

Anyone, then, who disparages this power of anger, as if it were in itself something unspiritual and therefore "to be mortified", acts the same as one who says the equivalent about "sensuality", "passion", and "desire"—both belittle the basic powers of our nature, both insult the Creator who, as the liturgy of the Church has said, "mar-

velously established the dignity of human nature".

Precisely with regard to overcoming licentiousness in pleasure, the power of growing angry assumes particular gravity.

Thomas is of the opinion that affirmation must
be stronger than negation. It is his opinion that the
degradation of a mental power must be capable of
being healed by the still undamaged core of some
other power. Therefore it must be possible to
overcome and, so to speak, quench the flabby licentiousness of a lecherous desire for pleasure, so
that a difficult task might be undertaken by the
willing resistance that the full power of anger can
engender.

The connection of the licentiousness of the desire
for pleasure with the indolent inability to get angry is the distinctive mark of complete and genuinely hopeless degeneration. It shows itself
wherever a social class, a people, or a culture is
ripe for ruin.

Hilaritas mentis, cheerfulness of the heart: the
Christian doctrine on living ties this concept to
nothing else as tightly as it does to the primal form
of all asceticism, fasting. This nexus is based in the

New Testament, in the instruction from the Lord that is proclaimed by the Church year after year at the beginning of Lent: "When you fast, do not put on a gloomy look" (Mt 6:16).

Augustine says that it does not at all matter what and how much one eats as long as the welfare of those with whom he has fellowship as well as one's own well-being and the exigencies of health are safeguarded. This should be the only condition: With what readiness and cheerfulness of heart can one do without things to consume if need or duty demands doing without?

If they are at all subjected to a truly moral evaluation, trespasses against the virtue of abstinence, namely, against the "reasonable order" in the matter of desiring food and drink, always strive to be taken very lightly. A clear and decisive affirmation of the Christian image of man, however, will plainly point out the destructive element that is inherent in the driving concern for what and how much food and drink to have. Thomas characterized this destructive element as *hebetudo sensus*, as the bluntness and dullness of the interior understanding in grasping spiritual realities. Is there not a certain causal relationship between the manifestation, on almost a daily basis as a matter of

course, of this dulling of the interior faculty and the equally everyday matter-of-fact quality of taking this dulling lightly?

Nothing shows the way to a correct understanding of humility so clearly as this: that humility and magnanimity not only are not mutually exclusive but also are near to one another and intimately connected; both together are in opposition to pride as well as to faintheartedness. What indeed does magnanimity mean? Magnanimity is the expansion of the spirit toward great things; one who expects great things of himself and makes himself worthy of it is magnanimous. The magnanimous person is to a certain extent "particular": he does not allow himself to become concerned with everything that comes along, but rather only with the great things that are suitable for him. Magnanimity seeks above all great glory: "The magnanimous person strives toward that which is worth the highest glory." In the *Summa Theologica* it is stated, "If one disdains glory in such a manner that he makes no effort to do that which merits glory, that action is blameworthy." On the other side, the magnanimous one is not broken by disgrace; he looks down on it as unworthy of himself. In general the magnanimous man regards with disdain anyone who is narrow-minded. He would

never be able to esteem another so highly that he
would do anything improper for that person's
sake. According to Thomas, the words of the
Psalm (15:4) apply to the magnanimous "disdain
for men" by the just man: "[He] looks with con-
tempt on the reprobate." Undaunted uprightness
is the distinctive mark of magnanimity, while
nothing is more alien to it than this: to be silent out
of fear about what is true. One who is magnanimous completely shuns flattery and hypocrisy,
both of which are the issue of a mean heart. The
magnanimous person does not complain, for his
heart does not permit him to be overcome by any
external evil. Magnanimity encompasses an un-
shakable firmness of hope, a plainly defiant certainty, and the thorough calm of a fearless heart.
The magnanimous person submits himself not to
the confusion of feelings or to any human being or
to fate—but only to God.

It is with some amazement that one learns that
this profile of magnanimity is traced line for line in
the *Summa Theologica* of St. Thomas. It was necessary to bring this to mind, for in the Treatise on
Humility it is stated several times that humility
does not conflict with magnanimity. One can now
consider what this sentence, uttered as a warning
and a precaution, truly means to say. It means
nothing else than this: that a "humility" that

would be too narrow and too weak to bear the inner tension of coexistence with magnanimity is indeed no humility.

There is a lust for seeing that perverts the original meaning of sight and casts a person into disorder. The meaning of sight is the perception of reality. However, the "concupiscence of the eyes" does not seek to perceive reality but rather just to see. Augustine notes that the "lust of the palate" does not attain satisfaction but only results in eating and drinking; the same holds true for *curiositas* (curiosity) and the "concupiscence of the eyes". In his book *Sein und Zeit* (Being and time), Martin Heidegger says, "The concern of this kind of sight is not about grasping the truth and knowingly living within it but is about chances for abandoning oneself to the world." The degradation into *curiositas* of the natural desire to see can thus be substantially more than a harmless confusion on the surface. It can be the sign of one's fatal uprooting. It can signify that a person has lost the capacity to dwell in his own self; that he, fleeing from himself, disgusted and bored with the waste of an interior that is burnt out by despair, seeks in a thousand futile ways with selfish anxiety that which is accessible only to the high-minded calm of a heart disposed to self-sacrifice and thus in mastery over

itself: the fullness of being. Since such a person does not truly live out of the wellspring of his being, he accordingly seeks, as again Heidegger says, in the "curiosity to which nothing is closed off", "the security of a would-be genuine 'living life' ".

The "concupiscence of the eyes" reaches its utmost destructive and extirpative power at the point where it has constructed for itself a world in its own image and likeness, where it has surrounded itself with the restlessness of a ceaseless film of meaningless objects for show and with a literally deafening noise of nothing more than impressions and sensations that roar in an uninterrupted chase around every window of the senses. Behind their papery façade of ostentation lies absolute nothingness, a "world" of at most one-day constructs that often become insipid after just one-quarter of an hour and are thrown out like a newspaper that has been read or a magazine that has been paged through; a world which, before the revealing gaze of a sound spirit uninfected by its contagion, shows itself to be like a metropolitan entertainment district in the harsh clarity of a winter morning: barren, bleak, and ghostly to the point of pushing one to despair.

Still, the destructive element of this disorder, born out of and shaped by illness, is found in the fact that this disorder obstructs the original power of man to perceive reality, that it renders a person unable not only to attain his own self but also to attain reality and truth.

If, therefore, a fraudulent world of this kind threatens to overrun and conceal the world of reality, then the cultivation of the natural desire to see assumes the character of a measure of self-preservation and self-defense. And then *studiositas* (diligence) means especially this: that a person resists the nearly inescapable temptation to indiscipline with all the power of selfless self-protection, that he radically closes off the inner space of his life against the pressingly unruly pseudoreality of empty sights and sounds—in order that, through and only through this asceticism of perception, he might safeguard or recoup that which truly constitutes man's living existence: to perceive the reality of God and of creation and to shape himself and the world by the truth that discloses itself only in silence.

"Man's being in the true sense is found in this: to exist in conformity with reason. Thus, when one behaves according to the truth, then it is said that

he is behaving himself." In a very particular way, unchastity destroys this self-possession and behaving oneself by man. Unchaste abandonment and prostitution of the soul to the sensual world wound the fundamental capacity of the moral person: to hearken in silence to the call of the real and out of this recollected silence within oneself to make the decision appropriate to the concrete situation of concrete action.

For us men and women of today, who are of the opinion that in order to know the truth one need only more or less strain one's brain, and who scarcely regard as sensible the concept of an ascesis of the intellect—for us, the deeply intrinsic connection that links the knowledge of truth to the condition of purity has vanished from our consciousness. Thomas notes that the firstborn daughter of unchastity is the blindness of spirit. Only one who wants nothing for himself, one who is not "interested" in an unobjective manner, can know the truth. An impure and selfishly degraded will for pleasure ruins both the decision-making power and the inmost resource of the soul to give silent heed to the discourse of reality.

To be open to the truth of real things and to live by perceived truth: these constitute the essence of the

moral person. Only one who sees and affirms this objective reality is also able to recognize how deeply the ruin penetrates that an unchaste heart allows to happen within itself.

Not only is the satisfaction of the spirit with the truth impossible without chastity, but even genuine sensual joy at sensual beauty is impossible. That sensual pleasure is not excluded by Christian precepts of living from the scope of the morally good (hence something more than just "permissible") need not be especially elaborated. However, that this pleasure should be made possible precisely through the virtue of discipline and moderation—that is a surprising thought. And yet, in the *Summa Theologica* of St. Thomas something to this effect can be read—although rather between and behind the lines of what is expressly said. It is stated there that, among animals, no desire springs from the activity of the other senses, such as the eye or the ear, that is not directed toward the satisfaction of hunger and the mating instinct; only for the sake of eating does the lion "rejoice" when he spies a deer or hears its call. Man, however, is able also to enjoy himself beyond the thing seen and heard *propter convenientiam sensibilium* (because of the harmony of the things perceived), on account of the sensory "propriety" inherent in the

object seen or heard, by which nothing else than sensual beauty is to be understood. One often reads and hears that, through lechery, a man sinks to the level of a beast—a comparison that should be used cautiously, since lechery (and also discipline) is something exclusively human; neither an angel nor a beast experiences it. Yet from this distinction the figure of speech does draw a good meaning: an unchaste will to pleasure has the tendency to relate the entirety of the sensory world, especially sensual beauty, to only sexual lust. Only a chaste sensuality can achieve true human capacity: to perceive sensual beauty, such as that of the human body, as beauty and to enjoy it, undisturbed and unstained by any selfish will to pleasure that befogs everything, for its own sake, *propter convenientiam sensibilium*. With good reason it is said: only he who has a pure heart can laugh in a freedom that creates freedom in others. It is no less true that only he who looks at the world with pure eyes experiences its beauty.

The high and truly noble propensity to render visible in a splendid manner a lofty thought in solemn celebration, by carrying out great achievements in imagery or construction—this virtue (for it is a virtue!) was called *magnificentia* by the Middle Ages; today we can no longer designate it with a

single word. However, in the same manner that *magnificentia* relates to "ordinary" generosity, which has its place in the daily pattern of needs and requests, so also does, says Thomas Aquinas, virginity relate to chastity.

Purity means that crystalline, morning-fresh artlessness and selflessness in relating to the world, as it becomes a reality in the person when the shock of a deep pain brings him to the limits of existence or when the nearness of death touches him. In Sacred Scripture it says, "Serious illness sobers the soul" (Sir 31:2); this sobriety belongs to the essence of purity. The most debated of Aristotle's tenets points in the same direction: tragedy achieves purification, catharsis. The *donum timoris*, the spiritual gift of fear, which Thomas subordinates to *temperantia*, also cleanses the disposition as the blessed experience of the innermost peril to the person; it has that purity as its fruit in virtue of which one renounces the selfish seeking after deceptive and false fulfillment. Purity is the unreserved openness of the entire being, from which alone the word can be spoken: "Behold the handmaid of the Lord" (Lk 1:38). This supreme realization of purity is expressed in one of the most perfect (and one of the most unknown) German poems in an image of immaculate beauty and

radiant authenticity: "Untroubled, the undaunted rose / stays open in hope" (Konrad Weiss).

Here a new depth becomes manifest: namely, that purity not only is the fruit of purification but also comprises in itself the readiness to accept God's purifications, perhaps terrible and deadly, with the brave openness of a trusting heart and so experiences its fertile and transforming power.

One of the scarcely examined principles from which our age's governing image of humanity is drawn asserts that it is not fitting for man to be afraid. In this attitude the waters from two sources are mingled. The one is Enlightenment liberalism, which relegates fearfulness to the realm of the un-essential, and, in its view of reality, room and place are assigned to fear only in an unessential sense. The other source is an un-Christian stoicism with a concealed link to impudence as well as to despair; it opposes the fearful things of existence, which are clearly seen, with defiant immovability, without fear, but also without hope.

Classical Western moral teaching does not conceive of denying that there is something fearsome in human existence; it is also remote from Christian moral teaching at all to say that man should or might not fear for the fearsome. Nonetheless, the Christian inquires after the *ordo timoris*, the order

of fear; he inquires about what is genuinely and ultimately fearsome; and it is his concern that he not fear things that are not at all truly and definitively fearsome, and likewise that he not regard as harmless something ultimately fearsome. What is truly fearsome, however, is nothing else than the possibility that man might separate himself from his ultimate Ground of Being voluntarily through his guilt. No person can bear this "serenely" or desire to incur it. This fearsomeness, which accompanies as a real possibility the life of every man, including the saints—the fearsomeness and this fear are not surmountable by any mode of "heroism"; on the contrary, this fear is a prerequisite for any genuine heroism.

The moral good is nothing else than the continuation and fulfillment of the natural tendencies of our being: in the fear of the Lord man's natural anxiety in the face of any diminishment in being or of annihilation is realized. If this natural human fear, contemplating nothingness, is not fulfilled through the fear of the Lord, then this anxiety erupts "unfulfilled" and destructive into the realm of spiritual and mental existence.

For man who, *in statu viatoris*, in the state of being on the way, experiences the essential creatureliness, the "not yet really existing being" of his

existence, there is only one appropriate answer to this experience. The answer cannot be despair—for the meaning of creaturely existence is not nothingness but rather is being, which means fulfillment. The response also cannot be the comfortable security of possessions—for the creature's "being as becoming" still borders in peril on nothingness. Both of these, despair and assurance of possession, militate against the truth of real things. The only answer that is suitable for man's authentic existential situation is hope. The virtue of hope is the first appropriate virtue of the *status viatoris*; it is the genuine virtue of the "not yet". In the virtue of hope, before all others, man understands and affirms that he is a creature, a creation of God.

Human existence and everything that immediately pertains to it have the structure of hope. We are *viatores*, on our way, "not yet" beings. Therein lie a No and a Yes. Who could say that he already possesses the being intended for him, that he has comprehended anything (to comprehend means to know something as much as it is knowable, to perceive something completely), that he has taken the measure of all existing things? And yet in contrast to this No there is a Yes: as much as our life and our knowledge are patchwork, they are none-

theless progress on the way—even though this way is also unending. This is just what we called the "structure of hope". In the virtue of hope, the eventual achievement of the original structure of human existence comes to pass.

Youthfulness and hope are associated with one another in multiple senses. They belong together, in both the natural and the supernatural realms. The form of a youth is the eternal symbol bearer of hope.

Natural hope springs from man's youthful power and dries up along with it. For supernatural hope, however, the reverse is true: it not only is not tied to being naturally young but also is itself the basis for a much more substantial youthfulness. It endows a person with a "not yet" that simply surpasses and is remote from the decline of natural powers of hope.

And the supernatural vigor of hope overflows and radiates even into the rejuvenated powers of natural hope. Nothing assures and establishes "eternal youth" (in the most literal sense of the word) as does the theological virtue of hope. It alone is able to provide man with the unalienable possession of that inner tension that is both relaxed and taut, that elasticity and agility, that stouthearted freshness, that resilient joyousness,

that composed bravery of confidence, which distinctly characterize a young person and thus make him lovable.

Since supernatural hope implants in man the new "future" of a simply inexhaustible "not yet", it establishes a new youthfulness, which can be destroyed only together with hope itself. In the two forms of hopelessness, in despair as well as in presumption, this youthfulness of the hoping person comes to nothing all the same, but in different ways: in despair, in the way of the senile; in presumption, in the way of the infantile.

In despair as in presumption, the truly human quality stiffens and congeals, and only hope is able to preserve it in radiant litheness. Both forms of hopelessness are in the real sense inhuman and deadly. "These two things kill the soul: despair and perverted hope", says Augustine.

Never can the natural man say as triumphantly as the Christian, "Things will end well for me." And never can the hope of the natural man hope for such an end as that of the Christian. Yet never can a pagan be tempted to such deep despair as a Christian and, so it appears, precisely the great Christians and the saints.

Hope and despair can each differ in depth. Above a hope that is rooted in the soul's innermost depth of being, there can be varieties of despair near the surface, so to speak. Yet they do not touch the more profound hope, and they have no definitive meaning. Furthermore, a person, who in the final analysis is in despair, can appear to be a thoroughgoing optimist in the penultimate concerns of existence, such as the naturally cultural, to others and to himself, as long as he is able to seal off radically the innermost chamber of despair, so that no cry of pain can erupt outward (and it speaks volumes that the contemporary man of the world has made a real art of this).

One of the most central concepts from the moral philosophy of the High Middle Ages is that of *acedia*, which we, very ambiguously and mistakenly, are accustomed to translate as "laziness". *Acedia*, however, means this: that man denies his effective assent to his true essence, that he closes himself to the demand that arises from his own dignity, that he is not inclined to claim for himself the grandeur that is imposed on him with his essence's God-given nobility of being. Out of such "laziness", then, according to the great teachers of the age of chivalry, something precisely opposed to indolence emerges, namely, leisurelessness, the inner

incapacity for leisure. Truly, an astounding explanation. However, anyone who understands the
structure of mental life will not find this associa-
tion to be absurd: that, therefore, the restlessness
of a suicidal frenzy for work can undergo an especially vehement increase precisely from a refusal
of oneself, precisely from a lack of desire for realization. Goethe indeed had something similar in
mind when he wrote to Zelter that it is character-
istic of the true to give too little to do, while the
false is what ignites industriousness.

What is involved in celebrating a feast? Without
doubt, more than a day off from work. It means
that a person, despite every mundane inconsis-
tency, indeed even through a veil of tears, affirms
the world's ultimate ground of meaning and
knows himself to be in agreement with it and em-
braced by it. To live out this affirmation, this assent, this recognition of oneself in an uncommon
manner—this is what men have always called a
feast. It is evident here that without gods there is
no feast, indeed, that the cultic celebration is the
prototype of the feast.

It is easy to flatter oneself that one hopes for eternal
life; however, it is hard truly to hope while in the
midst of temptations to despair. In the situation of

utmost bravery it becomes evident whether the
hope is authentic. No one knows more deeply
than one who is truly brave that and how greatly
hope is "virtue" and thus not "to be had" casually
and, as it were, "without charge"; no one experiences more clearly that the hope for eternal life is
a grace.

It can happen that, in a period of temptations to
despair, all inner prospects for a "happy ending"
grow dark. It can also happen that, for the person
confined to the natural, nothing else remains than
the hopeless bravery of the "heroic downfall". Indeed, this possibility will present itself as the only
one to the true gentleman, since he is just the one
who is able to forego soothing self-deception and
narcosis along with, as Ernst Jünger notes, the
"outlet of luck". In a word, it can also sometimes
happen that supernatural hope remains simply the
only possibility of hope at all. This is not meant
here in some kind of "eudaemonistic" sense; it is
not a question here of a concern for a final possibility of a subjective ability to be happy. The sentence from Sacred Scripture—"Even were he to
kill me, I have no other hope than [him]" (Job
13:15)—is remote from nothing so much as it is
from the eudaemonistic anxiety about happiness.
No, Christian hope is first and foremost an exis-

tential direction of man toward the perfection of his being, toward the fulfillment of his essence, thus toward his ultimate realization, toward the fullness of being (to which, to be sure, there also corresponds the fullness of fortune or rather of happiness).

If, then, as has been said, at times all natural hopes become meaningless, then that means that at times supernatural hope remains simply the only possibility for man to align himself toward Being. The despairing bravery of the "heroic downfall" is fundamentally nihilistic; it looks toward nothingness; it presumes that it is able to endure nothingness. The bravery of a Christian, however, thrives on the hope in life's abundance of reality, in eternal life, in a new heaven and a new earth.

D1577725